POT-

What It Is,
What It Does

by ANN TOBIAS

illustrated by

TOM HUFFMAN

GREENWILLOW BOOKS | NEW YORK

Printed in the United States of America   First Edition   1 2 3 4 5 6 7 8 9 10

Library of Congress Cataloging in Publication Data
Tobias, Ann. Pot, what it is what it does. (Greenwillow read-alone books)
Summary: An introduction to the basic facts about marijuana.
1. Marihuana—Psychological aspects—Juvenile literature.
2. Marihuana—Physiological effect—Juvenile literature.
[1. Marihuana] I. Huffman, Tom. II. Title. BF209.C3T6
613.8   78-10817 ISBN 0-688-80200-1   ISBN 0-688-84200-3 lib. bdg.

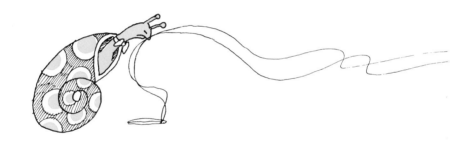

For S.C.H.
—A.T.

For Momma and Brian Thomas
—T.H.

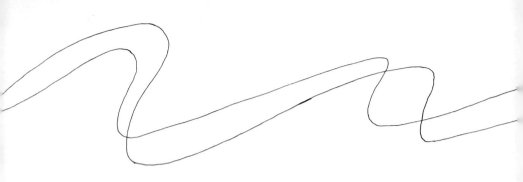

Contents

Introduction

You may have a friend
who uses pot.
He will tell you
using it is cool.
He will tell you
he knows a lot of people
who use it.
Some are adults,
some are teenagers,
and some are even children.
Most of them started
because their friends did.

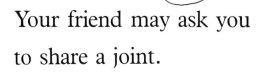

Your friend may ask you
to share a joint.
If he does, what will you say?

Knowing about pot—
   what it is,
   how it makes you feel,
   what it does to your body,
   what the law says about it—
will help you make the right choice
when and if you need to.

1 · Pot Is a Drug

A drug is a chemical
that changes the way you feel.
Drugs are most often used
to cure or prevent disease.
But they are not always used
in this way.

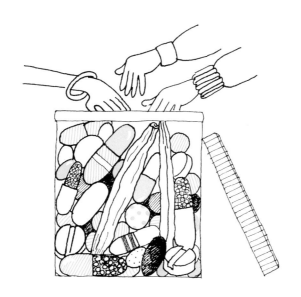

Some people take drugs
when they are not sick.
They take drugs over and over,
and their bodies and their minds
become used to them.
The time comes when
they cannot live
without drugs.

You may call pot
"marijuana" or "grass"
or "weed."
Whatever you call it,
pot is a drug.

Scientists have been
studying pot for years.
But it was hard to test
what they found.
Recently new ways to test pot
have been discovered.
And scientists are now learning
more about it every day.

2 • **What Is Pot?**

Pot is made from
the dried, chopped leaves
and flowers of a certain plant.
Its Latin name is
cannabis sativa.
It has two forms—
a male plant and a female.
They look almost the same.
But the leaves and flowers
of the female plant produce
a lot of sticky resin.

FEMALE   MALE

This resin contains
delta-9-tetrahydrocannabinol.
THC is a shorter name for it.

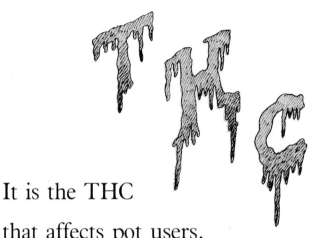

It is the THC

that affects pot users.

The male plant has less resin,

and so pot from the male plant

has very little THC.

That is why pot

from the male plant is weak,

and users don't like it.

3 · **Some History**

People have used pot
for thousands of years.
It was first used in China
as a medicine.

Pot was thought to cure
weakness, gout, rheumatism,
and forgetfulness.
After hundreds of years
pot was used less and less
as a medicine.
But its use as a drug had
spread to the rest
of the world.

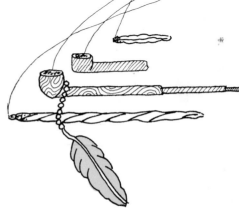

Depending on where they lived,
people mixed pot in tea and
other drinks, or ate it in foods,
or smoked it in cigarettes.

Pot was brought to the
United States in the 1920s.
Workers on the docks
in New Orleans were
the first to use it.
Some of the jazz musicians
living in New Orleans
at that time used it too.

They said it helped them
to play better.
They smoked it in cigarettes
they called reefers.
Now these cigarettes
are called joints.
Today most users smoke pot
in pipes or joints.

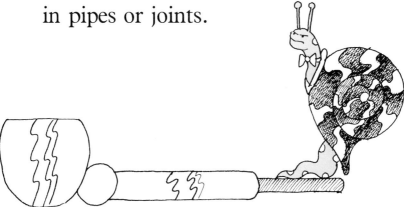

4. **What Is Smoking Pot Like?**

Your friend who uses pot
may tell you he likes
getting high or stoned.
That means for a few hours
he feels pleased with himself
and with his world.

He says time and space
seem to change for him.
He says he is more aware
of touch, taste, smell,
sight, and sound.
He says he does not worry
about his job or his homework
or getting along with his friends.

But someone else may try pot
and not like it at all.
It may make him feel
sick to his stomach
and throw up.
It may make him feel tired,
sad, and scared.
He may get dizzy
or even faint.

Another friend may tell you
pot had no effect on him
when he tried it.
Often beginning pot smokers
do not feel any effects
when they first use it.

5 · How Does Pot Work?

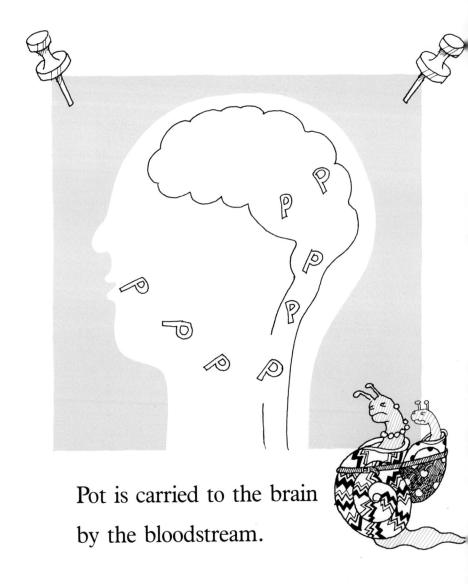

Pot is carried to the brain by the bloodstream.

The THC in pot shuts off

the part of the brain

that controls the senses

and memory.

Your friend who says

he feels good

when he smokes pot

does not know that

until the pot wears off,

a part of his mind

has stopped working.

You may know someone
who says he feels the same
the day after he smoked pot
as he did before he used it.
He will tell you
there are no aftereffects.
But scientists say that is not so.

It takes days for pot
to leave the body.
During that time pot smokers

may feel tired and sad.
They may have trouble sleeping.
They do not know why.
Days have passed
since they were high.
They do not connect
the way they feel
with the pot they smoked.

6 · Can You Tell If Someone Is on Pot?

Let's say you have a friend
who has just started using pot.
At first you do not see
any changes in him.

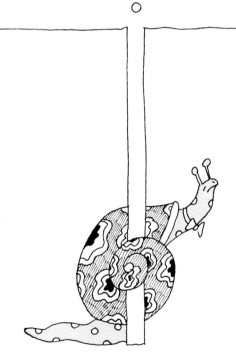

Often users of other drugs
show the effects of drug-taking
as soon as they begin.
But not people on pot.

That is because pot
acts on the body and the mind
more slowly than other drugs.
THC from pot is stored
in tissues of the body
for about a week.
If a pot user has one joint
once or twice a week,
his body is never free of pot.

After a while the THC builds
up and attacks his body.
And in a few weeks or months
his body and his behavior
show signs that he is on drugs.

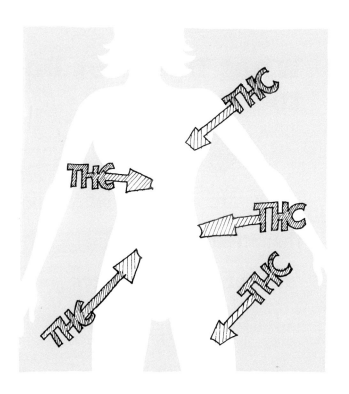

7 · **What Does Pot Do to Your Body?**

There are scientists who believe

that steady use of even

one or two joints a week

is harmful.

Scientists say:

➤ The use of pot
for two or three years
will damage the brain.
The user will have trouble
remembering and concentrating
for the rest of his life.

➤ Pot attacks the lungs and throat.
Pot smokers cough a lot.
They develop lung diseases easily.
Lung cancer may be caused
by pot smoke.

Pot keeps blood cells from
forming and growing properly.
Red blood cells are needed
to carry oxygen
to all parts of the body.
White blood cells are needed
to fight disease.

Pot may cause
birth defects in babies.

Pot may reduce sperm in men.

 Pot may keep reproductive systems in teenagers from developing normally.

 Pot prevents normal growth.

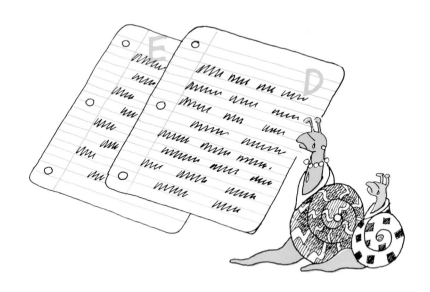

8 · **How Does Pot Affect Your Behavior?**

Just as pot changes your body,

it may change

how you behave.

☞ Teachers say that students on pot
make low grades.

☞ Parents say that children on pot
do not seem to care
about the people around them.

☞ Employers say that people on pot
show no ambition or drive.

☞ And psychologists say that
young people on pot
are hiding from their problems.

9 • Other Dangers

Pot affects a person's
timing and coordination.
Driving a car, riding a bike,
skateboarding,
and many things
you do every day
become dangerous.

Sometimes there are harmful chemicals such as PCP mixed in with pot.

Poisons sprayed on *cannabis* can make users sick.

10 • The Law

Using pot is against the law
in almost every part of the world.
In the United States
punishments for using pot
are different depending on

- which state you live in,
- how much pot you are caught with,
- whether you are buying it
  or selling it,
- where you smoke it.

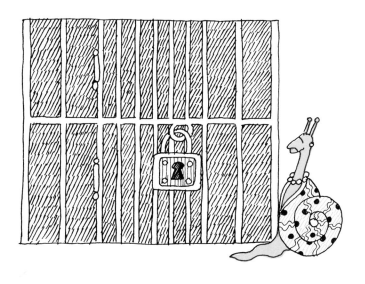

But using it is always illegal.

In the 1960s

thousands of young people

were arrested for using pot.

They were given long jail terms

and heavy fines.

The lives and careers of many

were ruined.

The public came to feel
the law was too strict.
By the late 1970s
eleven states had voted
to lighten the punishment
for using pot.
Although the punishments
are now lighter in those states,
it is still illegal to use pot
in any state.

It is illegal to grow pot
almost everywhere in the world.
In the United States people
have been arrested and jailed
for growing it in gardens
or windowboxes.

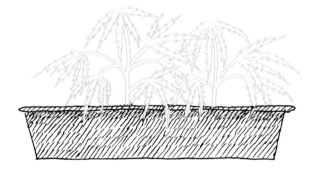

Most of the pot used in this country
is smuggled in from other countries
where it is grown illegally.

11 · **Your Decision**

From earliest times man
has looked for an easy way
to escape for a while
from his everyday problems.

During the 1960s some people
thought they had found
their escape in pot because

It was cheap.

It was easy to find.

Everyone seemed to accept it.

It was believed safe.

Today we know pot is not safe.
We know more about what it does
to our bodies and to our minds.
And we know that using it
is against the law.

Now that you know these facts,
what will you say to your friend
when he asks you to share a joint?

You will have to think about
how you want to treat
your body and your mind.
You will have to think about
obeying the law.
No one will tell you what to do.
The choice will be yours.

ANN TOBIAS knows that many of today's young people are going to be asked the questions this book answers. She knows that it is vital that both adults and children face this fact together, and that help and support be available.

Ann Tobias grew up in the Midwest and West, and came to New York City after graduation from college. She worked for several years in a major publishing house and taught a course in creative writing. She and her family live in Chappaqua, New York.

TOM HUFFMAN was born in Cincinnati, Ohio, and grew up in Lexington, Kentucky. He holds a B.A. from the University of Kentucky and attended the School of Visual Arts in New York City. He is a free-lance artist whose drawings have appeared in *Glamour, Seventeen, Cricket,* and other national magazines. Among the children's books he has illustrated are *Alcohol—What It Is, What It Does* (also a Greenwillow Read-alone Book); *What's in the Name of Birds; Your Brain Power; Dollars and Cents;* and *Ink, Ark, and All That.*